SilverTip

Extreme Weather

by Jane Parks Gardner

Consultant: Jordan Stoleru, Science Educator

BEARPORT
PUBLISHING

Minneapolis, Minnesota

Credits

Cover and title page, © elroce/Adobe Stock, © AegeanBlue/iStock, and © James BO Insogna/ Shutterstock; 5T, © Ryan DeBerardinis/Shutterstock; 5MT, © i am adventure/Shutterstock; 5MB, © Igumnova Irina/Shutterstock; 5B, © Alaskagirl8821/Shutterstock; 7, © Siberian Art/ Shutterstock; 8, © BearFotos/Shutterstock; 9, © milehightraveler/iStock; 11, © TWStock/Shutterstock; 13, © Wildeside/Shutterstock; 15, © ND700/Shutterstock; 16–17, © MainlanderNZ/Shutterstock; 19, © Artsiom P/Shutterstock; 20–21, © Arthur Villator/Shutterstock; 23, © John Weast/Getty; 24–25, © John Normile/Getty; 27, © Petro Perutskyi/Shutterstock; 28, © VectorMine/Shutterstock.

Bearport Publishing Company Product Development Team

President: Jen Jenson; Director of Product Development: Spencer Brinker; Managing Editor: Allison Juda; Associate Editor: Naomi Reich; Associate Editor: Tiana Tran; Art Director: Colin O'Dea; Designer: Elena Klinkner; Designer: Kayla Eggert; Product Development Assistant: Owen Hamlin.

STATEMENT ON USAGE OF GENERATIVE ARTIFICIAL INTELLIGENCE
Bearport Publishing remains committed to publishing high-quality nonfiction books. Therefore, we restrict the use of generative AI to ensure accuracy of all text and visual components pertaining to a book's subject. See BearportPublishing.com for details.

Library of Congress Cataloging-in-Publication Data is available at www.loc.gov or upon request from the publisher.

ISBN: 979-8-88916-522-4 (hardcover)
ISBN: 979-8-88916-529-3 (paperback)
ISBN: 979-8-88916-535-4 (ebook)

For more information, write to Bearport Publishing, 5357 Penn Avenue South, Minneapolis, MN 55419.

Contents

Wild Weather

Hurricanes rip through **coastal** cities. Meanwhile, heat waves and **droughts** dry out other parts of the world. Wildfires burn up old forests. And blizzards knock out power, leaving whole communities in freezing darkness.

Weather is getting more extreme. Why? A big reason is **climate change**.

Weather is what is happening in a moment. It may be rainy or sunny. The climate is the usual weather in a place. It is what can be expected based on patterns from the past.

Planet Greenhouse

Earth is the only planet that is the right temperature for life. This is in part because of something called the **greenhouse effect**.

How does it work? Sunlight makes its way to Earth. Dark-colored things on Earth **absorb** the sunlight. This makes heat. **Greenhouse gases** around Earth trap much of the heat in.

The greenhouse effect makes Earth's average temperature about 59 degrees Fahrenheit (15 degrees Celsius). Without it, our planet would be closer to -0.4°F (-18°C).

Atmosphere

A lot of heat is trapped by the atmosphere.

Heat comes to Earth.

Some heat is absorbed.

Some heat escapes.

Some greenhouse gases are made in nature. However, humans also add a lot of them to the air. These gases are let out when we burn **fossil fuels** to power our cars, homes, and factories. The added greenhouse gases trap even more heat. This has led to more extreme climate change.

Humans and other animals breathe out carbon dioxide. Methane is let off when waste breaks down. These natural sources of greenhouse gases alone would keep Earth warm enough for life.

Transportation adds more greenhouse gases to the air than any other activity.

Getting Hot

One of the most obvious signs of climate change is global warming. Earth is heating up. Since 1880, the planet has warmed by about 2°F (1°C).

Across the globe, many areas are getting hotter. Heat records are being shattered. And stretches of extreme heat are lasting longer.

Heat waves are periods of unusually hot weather that last for more than two days. They can be very dangerous. Extreme heat is the deadliest kind of weather event.

As it gets hotter, some places get drier. Droughts are periods with less than normal amounts of rain. This kind of weather dries out plants, including food crops.

There have always been some droughts on Earth. But global warming is making them more common. It's also making droughts last longer.

Droughts can easily lead to other problems. **Dust storms** start when strong winds pick up dried-out soil. Wildfires burn hotter and more quickly during extreme droughts.

Wet and Wild

While some places are getting drier, climate change is making others wetter. Areas that do get rain are getting a lot more of it.

Higher temperatures take more water out of the earth. All this moisture collects in clouds. Eventually, the water falls down again as rain.

Warmer air holds more water than cooler air. So, warm, wet clouds let out more rain. Heavy rains can damage crops. Sometimes, they cause flooding and mudslides.

Water on Land

As the planet warms, its ice is melting. Water from melting ice sheets goes into the oceans. This extra water has caused **sea levels** to rise. Places along the coast are flooding more often. Some low islands have already been covered.

Flooding is forcing some people from their homes. Communities on flooded islands have had to move away. They are climate **refugees**. These are people who have to leave their homes because of climate change.

Hurricane Hazard

Warmer oceans also create more hurricanes. These storms form when warm water from the oceans rises into the air.

Winds pull the warm, wet air up. Cool air rushes in to replace the rising air. This creates a spinning motion.

About 90 percent of the planet's extra heat goes into the oceans. From 1901 through 2020, the oceans got about 1.5°F (0.8°C) hotter. This has created more energy for stronger hurricanes.

The spinning storms gain energy. Eventually, they become hurricanes.

Hurricanes bring heavy rain to coastal cities. Strong winds push water from the oceans onto shore. This powerful rush of water is called a **storm surge**. It can lead to deadly flooding.

Storm surge waters can be more than 30 feet (10 m) high. Surge water often rushes onto land quickly. The fast flooding can kill people who think the danger of a hurricane has passed.

Brrr!

The warming planet can even impact winter weather. Strong winds usually hold very cold air over the Arctic. The chill stays near the top of the globe. But climate change is impacting Earth's winds. Warmer air can weaken the winds holding Arctic air in place. This sends the cold south.

Arctic air is making its way to places not used to cold weather. People and other animals living in the area can be hurt. Many plants freeze to death.

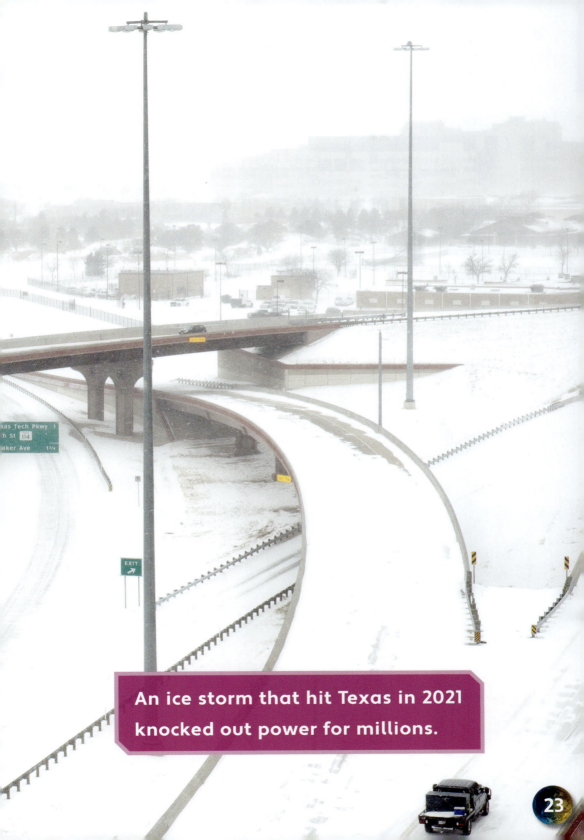

An ice storm that hit Texas in 2021 knocked out power for millions.

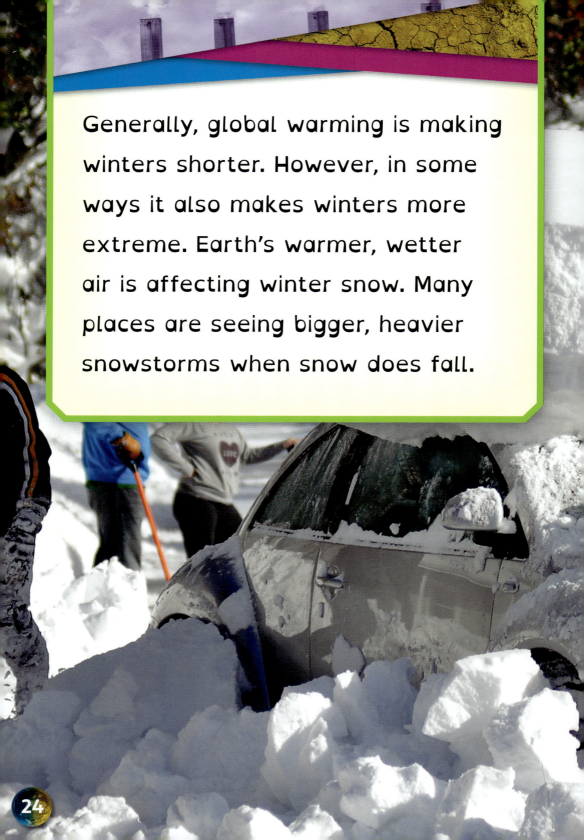

Generally, global warming is making winters shorter. However, in some ways it also makes winters more extreme. Earth's warmer, wetter air is affecting winter snow. Many places are seeing bigger, heavier snowstorms when snow does fall.

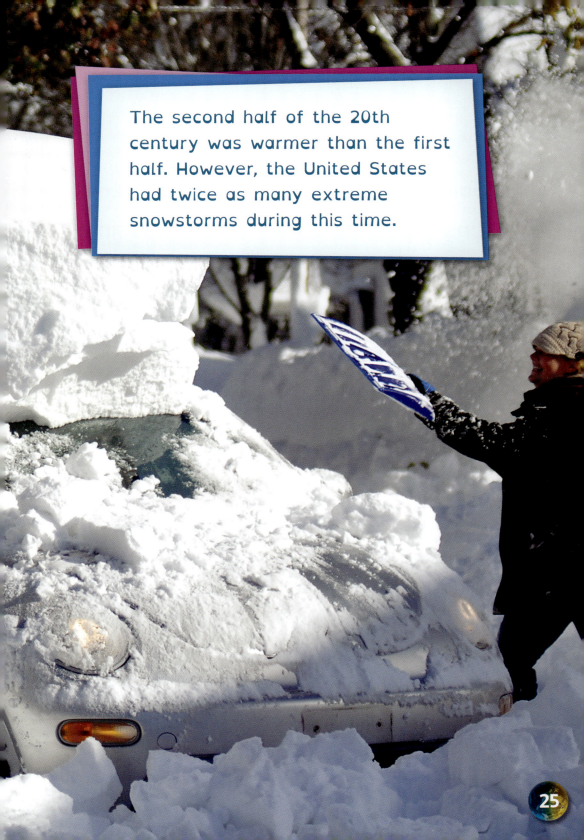

The second half of the 20th century was warmer than the first half. However, the United States had twice as many extreme snowstorms during this time.

What Can We Do?

As Earth's climate changes, weather is getting more extreme. This is causing major storms. But it's not too late to do something. Burning fewer fossil fuels will help slow climate change. So will finding other ways to power our world. Together, we can make a difference.

We can get power from the sun and the wind. These forms of energy do not let out as many greenhouse gases. They are often called green energy. That is because they are better for Earth.

We take in power from the sun by using solar panels.

Extreme Hurricanes

Hurricanes have gotten stronger as the climate has changed. They form over water in warm, wet weather. How does this happen?

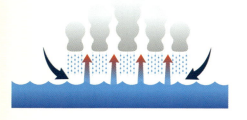

1 Warm, wet air rises up. Cool air rushes in to replace it.

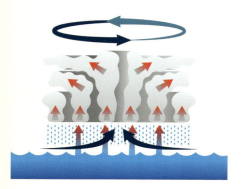

2 Clouds form. The storm starts to spin with the movement of the air.

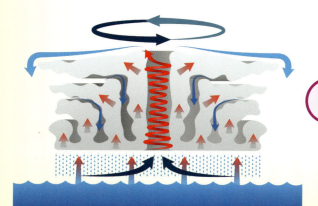

3 The storm gains energy. When it picks up enough speed, it becomes a hurricane.

★ SilverTips for **REVIEW**

Review what you've learned. Use the text to help you.

Define key terms

climate change
droughts
global warming

greenhouse effect
hurricanes

Check for understanding

Explain how the greenhouse effect works and the ways in which humans are impacting this natural process.

How has climate change affected rainstorms and hurricanes?

What are the impacts of climate change on winter weather?

Think deeper

What are some ways you have seen climate change impact weather where you live?

★ SilverTips on **TEST-TAKING**

- **Make a study plan.** Ask your teacher what the test is going to cover. Then, set aside time to study a little bit every day.

- **Read all the questions carefully.** Be sure you know what is being asked.

- **Skip any questions** you don't know how to answer right away. Mark them and come back later if you have time.

Glossary

absorb to soak up something

climate change changes in the usual weather patterns around Earth, including the warming of the air and oceans, due to human activities

coastal having to do with the area of land that runs along an ocean

droughts long periods of dry weather with much less rain or snow than usual

dust storms huge windstorms that blow dust and dirt across many miles

fossil fuels energy sources, such as coal, oil, and gas, made from the remains of plants and animals that died millions of years ago

greenhouse effect the warming of Earth because of heat trapped close to the planet by gases in the atmosphere

greenhouse gases carbon dioxide, methane, and other gases that trap heat around Earth

refugees people who have been forced to leave their homes

sea levels the average height of the oceans' surfaces

storm surge a rush of water coming onto land due to a storm or hurricane

Read More

Faust, Daniel R. *Global Warming (Climate Change: Need to Know).* Minneapolis: Bearport Publishing Company, 2024.

Kerry, Isaac. *Climate Change and Extreme Weather (Spotlight on Climate Change).* Minneapolis: Lerner Publications, 2023.

Ungvarsky, Janine. *The Weather Encyclopedia (Science Encyclopedias).* Minneapolis: ABDO Publishing, 2023.

Learn More Online

1. Go to **www.factsurfer.com** or scan the QR code below.

2. Enter "**Extreme Weather**" into the search box.

3. Click on the cover of this book to see a list of websites.

Index

About the Author

Jane Parks Gardner has written more than 60 books about science. Her favorite topics to write about include plate tectonics, climate change, and marine animals (especially octopuses)!